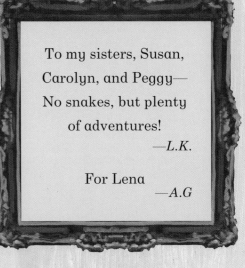

To my sisters, Susan,
Carolyn, and Peggy—
No snakes, but plenty
of adventures!
—L.K.

For Lena
—A.G

Ω

Published by
PEACHTREE PUBLISHERS
1700 Chattahoochee Avenue
Atlanta, Georgia 30318-2112
www.peachtree-online.com

Text © 2009 by Leslie Kimmelman
Illustrations © 2009 by Adam Gustavson

The illustrations were rendered in oil on prepared paper.

Printed and bound in China
10 9 8 7 6 5 4 3 2 1
First Edition

Library of Congress Cataloging-in-Publication Data

Kimmelman, Leslie.
  Mind Your Manners, Alice Roosevelt! / written by Leslie
Kimmelman ; illustrated by Adam Gustavson.
      p. cm.
  Summary: A brief, fictionalized account of what life was
like for Theodore Roosevelt during his political career, with
his oldest daughter, Alice, a strong-willed and somewhat wild
young woman, who loved to do things that shocked the
public, even when she lived in the White House.
  ISBN 978-1-56145-492-1 / 1-56145-492-3
  1. Longworth, Alice Roosevelt, 1884-1980—Juvenile fiction.
  2. Roosevelt, Theodore, 1858-1919—Juvenile fiction. [1.
Longworth, Alice Roosevelt, 1884-1980—Fiction. 2. Roosevelt,
Theodore, 1858-1919—Fiction.] I. Gustavson, Adam, ill. II.
Title.
  PZ7.K56493Al 2009
  [E]—dc22
                                                   2008052837

Mind your Manners, Alice Roosevelt!

Written by Leslie Kimmelman and illustrated by Adam Gustavson

PEACHTREE
ATLANTA

Teddy Roosevelt, the twenty-sixth president of the United States, was a strong and clever man. He could handle almost anything.

Teddy knew how to handle sickness. He had been so sick as a child that he had to be schooled at home. He exercised hard, and little by little his health improved. From then on, even when he got sick, he never complained.

But Teddy Roosevelt *didn't* always know how to handle his oldest daughter, Alice.

Alice, get down from that sofa!

Alice, why can't you dress like everybody else?

Teddy knew how to handle fighting. During the Spanish-American War, "Rough Rider" Roosevelt led a famous charge up San Juan Hill.

Teddy knew how to handle New York. He was governor of the state for two years.

But Teddy Roosevelt *didn't* always know
how to handle his oldest daughter, Alice.

Teddy knew how to handle being vice president of the United States.

Then, when President McKinley died suddenly in 1901,

Teddy took charge and learned how to handle being president.

But Teddy Roosevelt *didn't* always know how to handle his oldest daughter, Alice.

Alice, we don't eat asparagus with gloves on.

Alice, that's not how you ride a bicycle.

Alice, MIND YOUR MANNERS!

As president, Teddy knew how to handle business leaders.

"Speak softly and carry a big stick," he liked to say.

Teddy was tough.

Teddy knew how to handle the Russians and the Japanese

when they couldn't stop fighting each other.

Teddy got them to shake hands and make up.

He got a Nobel Peace Prize for that.

Teddy knew how to handle the planet.

He helped to create a system of national parks

so that the land and wildlife were protected.

But Teddy Roosevelt *didn't* always know
how to handle his oldest daughter, Alice.

He told her that while she lived under his roof,
she had to obey his rules. What did Alice do?
She simply decided to spend her time *over* his roof!

Alice was among the first women in America
to drive a car, and she was also
one of the speediest!

Other times the president acted more like a commander in chief. Once he was told that his younger children were using mirrors to bounce sunlight through windows of government offices, interrupting important work.

Teddy had a staff member use flags to signal back a message:

A T T A C K
ON THIS BUILDING
MUST IMMEDIATELY
CEASE

But Alice's idea of fun was sometimes

just too much for him.

Teddy Roosevelt knew how to handle the White House pets.
It was a good thing, because there were a lot of them—
though not all at the same time.

Eli Yale

Loretta

Manchu

Josiah

A kangaroo rat

Sailor Boy

Skip

Pete

Algonquin

A one-legged rooster

Tom Quartz
and Slippers

Admiral Dewey, Jr.
and Father G. Grady

Jonathan Edwards

...and several horses

Teddy was used to wild animals, too. So you would think
that handling a snake—actually holding it in his hands—
wouldn't be hard for him, and it wasn't. But handling Alice
and her pet snake was not so easy. The snake's name was
Emily Spinach: Emily after Alice's very thin Aunt Emily,
and Spinach for her green color.

Alice took Emily Spinach with her wherever she went.
Sometimes she draped the snake around her neck and shoulders.
Other times she carried Emily around in her pocketbook.

Not all of the White House guests appreciated the snake.
"She's quite harmless," Alice tried to tell them.
Secretly, she enjoyed the commotion.

Sometimes Emily escaped. She liked to hide in the State Dining Room, where she had lots of company. But at one time or another, she probably got lost in every single room of the White House!

"Why don't you do something about Alice?"
a friend asked the president.

"I can do one of two things," answered Teddy
Roosevelt. "I can be president of the United States
or I can control Alice. I cannot possibly do both."

Luckily for the country, Princess Alice

(for that was Alice Roosevelt's nickname)

was already mostly grown up. She got married and left the White House.

Her father didn't have to handle her anymore.

Teddy Roosevelt concentrated on being president of the United States.

He did a good job of it, too.

He was one of our best and most-loved presidents.

And Alice?

She lived for many, many more years in Washington, D.C.,

long after her father had left the White House.

Even when she was very old, she still didn't mind her manners.

At her tea parties and her dinner parties, she would seat people who

didn't like each other side by side! Usually right next to her favorite pillow:

In fact, no one ever quite learned how to handle Alice—

but for ninety-six years, she sure did know how to have a good time.

Author's Note

The places, people, animals, and activities in the story are based on fact. The president really made the remark about how hard it was to control Alice. Emily Spinach, a harmless green garter snake, did have the unfortunate habit of disappearing around the White House—but whether it actually got lost in the president's Oval Office is anybody's guess.

About Alice

Alice Roosevelt (1884–1980) was the only child of Roosevelt's first marriage. Her mother, Alice Hathaway Lee, died in childbirth. Several years later, Teddy Roosevelt married Edith Carow and the two of them had five more children.

Teddy Roosevelt's family, c.1903, left to right:
Quentin, Teddy, Theodore Jr., Archie, Alice,
Kermit, Edith, Ethel
(PHOTOGRAPH COURTESY OF THE LIBRARY OF CONGRESS)

Alice was a little bit wild. She liked to shock people; Emily Spinach was one way of doing that. Alice also liked to go to parties. The public enjoyed hearing about Alice's antics. The song, "Alice, Where Art Thou Going?" became a bestseller after it came out in 1906. Alice continued her wild behavior after leaving the White House. She lived to be ninety-six years old, entertaining and being entertained by a great many presidents.

Whatever happened to Emily Spinach? Alice discovered the snake dead in its box home in the White House one day. The mystery of how Emily Spinach died remains unsolved a hundred years later.

Pictured on the previous spread:
Robert F. Kennedy, Alice Roosevelt Longworth, J. Edgar Hoover,
Richard M. Nixon, Lyndon B. Johnson, Lady Bird Johnson